MW01613057

A Fantastic Journey
of Time and Thought

Carl Vernon Bogle

A publication of

Eber & Wein Publishing

Pennsylvania

A Fantastic Journey of Time and Thought

Copyright © 2016 by Carl Vernon Bogle

Library of Congress
Cataloging in Publication Data

ISBN 978-1-60880-567-9

Proudly manufactured in the United States of America by

Eber & Wein Publishing
Pennsylvania

Contents

Poems...1

    My Mother 3

    The Intimate Rose 4

    Inspiration 5

    The Shadow 6

    Sorrow...7

    Raindrops 8

    Rainbow 9

    Memories 10

    Lady 11

    Imperilous Venture.....................................12

    The Beauty of the Rose 13

    Voices in the Sea 14

    The Stars 15

    The Lament of the Dead............................16

    Evil's Incognito 17

Short Stories...19

    A Small English Drama.............................21

    An English Story Using Their Words.......23

    A Curious Mystery: A Short Scottish Story ...24

    The Unread Letter 25

    The Forgotten Cathedral 26

    A Story of Hawaii.......................................28

    The Sea Monster 29

    The Tie and the New Car: A Tearful Christmas Story ...30

    Two Lonely Souls 32

Theories and Dreams 35

    Could These Theories Be the Answer Behind
       the "Mona Lisa's Mystic Smile?" 37

    What If It Were Possible to Move Things by Sight?......38

    A Cure for Leprosy.....................................39

Our Corrupt Legal System: One Instance......................40
The Cave: An Impossible Dream...................................41
Essays...43
Who We Are and Why We Are Different Each Day..... 45
A Sequel to Who We Are, And Why We Are Different
    Each Day... 46
Broken Blossoms: A 1919 Silent Movie Summary 47
Youth: Just Exactly What Is It?.....................................49

Poems

My Mother

She was my mother.
Just a lowly housewife was she.
Our existence was of a very poor fare;
When I was a lad, with mother and dad.

Sharecroppers were we of lowly estate.
Barely eking out a living in times less great.
Mother, a school teacher, wanted to be;
But very little education had she.

She and dad were wed in 1937.
As time went by, children numbered were seven.
We had no car; no luxuries at all.
Just hard work and toil; as dad worked the soil.

Mom was a friend to every stranger;
Because in those days there was very little danger.
Willie Roberta Walls was her name;
Always longing for something better, but it never came.

As time went on, for us times got worse.
For in 1954, a great flame burst.
A horrible house fire, one cold wintry day;
February 11 it was; taking everything we loved forever away.

About 60 seconds later the roof of our house fell in;
She and 3 others barely made it to the road that day, a scene so grim.
Such things as this, we all mostly endured in nearly every instance;
Of our meager existence.

My mother.
I love her.
Like old songs say,
There is no other like our mother.

8-4-2016

The Intimate Rose

A rose has always been a symbol of radiance rare,
a beautiful flower that no other can compare.

A symbol of love, of peace,
a token of expression, the heart it does reach.

Many a knight of the "dead days of yore"
has bravely emblazoned it on his shield, while cannons roar.

A rainbow of color, of exquisite compassion in battle sore,
of gentle tenderness into the wilderness the rose reigns forevermore.

10-19-2014

Inspiration

Inspiration is like a gift from on high
without a shadow or a sigh.
It is that certain something, an elan that has many meanings,
a creation, an idea, a twinkling, an intimate thought,
a bright hue, searching for something that is true.
To be inspired is an artistic belief,
a heavenly vision without intrusion,
a new beginning, a freshness, a poetic enchantment
looming beautifully, an animation
born anew, more than sensation.
A certain beauty from afar,
finding out just who we are.

5-7-2015

The Shadow

The shadow is a mysterious thing.
It follows us wherever we go
as long as there is light.
This is quite a ruse.
By contrast, this umbra image
makes one go into a muse.

It is caused by irradiated radiation.
That in itself is quite a sensation.
It lengthens at noon,
creating its full image
not a moment too soon.

Then it begins to deviate,
decreasing in size,
still following its owner
before its demise.

"Me and my shadow," as an old song states.
Where do you go? Why do you dissipate?
Your mysterious ways like a disappearing haze,
next day you appear anew all over and then
start your mystery all over again.

5-11-2015

Sorrow

Sorrow, oh sorrow, you are a dark foe.
You creep into our lives, bringing pain and woe.
You are no friend, you loathsome creature.
Why do you follow us with all your dark features?
You have been with us since the fall of Adam,
a shadow of gloom lurking there, like the atom.
There is no light wherever you dwell.
You bring no comfort, you creation of hell.
Musty and dank like an old basement,
there you linger in all your encasement.
Must you always have your way, you dark folly?
Black as you are and never jolly?
Unless we are saved by Jesus' blood, and through Him only,
can we ever lose you, ere we be forever lonely.

6-17-2015

Raindrops

Raindrops, raindrops, pitter patter, pitter patter
on my rooftop.
Like little winged fairies in their whirling dances of mirth,
fall little raindrops in your cascading glide to Earth.
A lovely sound you make as you tumble to and fro,
falling from the heavens to distant Earth below—
God's refreshing way of saying
Hello, Earth, hello!
You shine in your sparkling gleam
as a thought in a dream.
Your dance prevails, and then you stop
to play another day, pretty little raindrops.

4-19-2015

Rainbow

Rainbow low in the sky,
Your gleaming beauty dazzles the eye.
Your beautiful prism colors
Of red, yellow, and blue
Strike a chord of harmony
That beams so true.

Rainbow, rainbow, in your radiant glow,
An arc of beauty to us you show.
With an aura of color by God divine,
Your spectral light by His design.

Rainbow, rainbow, where did you go?
You were here a while ago.
So now you fade and disappear
By His light divine and to us so dear.

Memories

Many, many years ago by a long since deserted road stands remnants of my childhood and the griefs we had to bear.

There sits on the boards of an ancient creaky porch one who is dear to me. The sparkle in her eyes has long since lost its glow.

Ah! Yes, my memory still wanders back to those faded days of yore, and of my curiosities, and of that fond ever-more. For hidden in the "vaults of time" that ne'er more can be, just memories that kindle the flame of longing.

Just dust and cobwebs decorate the site of my birth-place, and all my child-like pleasures have vanished therein. Where once there was gold, time has covered this dear old lady's hair with gray. Just sitting there looking skyward and dreaming of her "castle in the air."

But we must be realistic. For this life is only lent to us, and the "Sweet Bird of Youth" soon flies away.

7-14-66

Lady

Upon one summer's day in the merry month of May, I chanced to meet a maiden fair with flowers in her hair, with sparkling eyes, a turned-up nose, and cheeks like the blushing rose.

She looked as flowers do—ere nature kisses them with her dew—with silken hair and trailing gown that hovers gently upon the ground. This beautiful lady with heart so true, a lovelier creature "I never knew."

Her movements so graceful and charm so sweet—to hush! the murmur, of the brook so meek. Her eyes so radiantly aglow, for others to tease her would vex me so. A creature of heavenly virtues, she reminds me of Venusian goddesses.

The bewitching smile, the innocent face, reveals the fire of her charm and grace. Ever flitting so gaily about, the fields and woodlands so firmly asprout.

If fate besought to bear her away should crush me beyond all mortal dismay. Mere thought of it makes me shudder and despair, for to steal "yon fair damsel away would make mine heart wither and decay."

But anon, oh to anon came the fatal day when her pulse ceased its beating: the cold hand of death had struck its final blow. 'Twas nothing more to do but place her in the cold, cold annals of the earth below.

The endless memories shall linger forever. But there comes a time when we must sever that whom we love so dear.

1-13-67

11

Imperilous Venture

Soaring gracefully in the perilous blue with "laughter silvered wings"

like a giant bird circling the heavens,

its silent roar of mighty engines throbs in the realm of space.

The pilot is ever aware of its awesome power, but one whisper from God could down it like thunderous explosions, fall towers.

The wrath of the invisible, angry at the machine for invading their domain,

sends it plummeting downward to a gruesome death.
But NO! It is not to be.
Being trained for any emergency,
the pilot makes the giant bird regain its course.
Man has won over matter this time, but there shall be others.

3-17-67

The Beauty of the Rose

Nestled in her innocence the elegance of her simplicity,
"The Flower of Love," the cherished flower of romance, grows.

The beauty of the rose, the inspiration of song,
its veil of happiness reigns amid the throng of envy and eternal
   scowls of wrong.

Her petals so fair, her nectar so inviting,
extending ever the blossoming bed of comfort to the lonely,
and the weary.

To gaze upon this flower is to tame the wildest creature.
A peaceful hand of affection, to cultivate to perfection,
is the beauty of the rose.

5-4-67

Voices in the Sea

Enchanting voices whisper silently, gliding faintly oe'r sun-kissed
   waves
to disappear o'er lonely, ocean graves.

They cast their spell amid the wretched tombs
and haunt the fallen bodies buried in the gloom.

The voices change their tone and swell their loathsome sound,
disturbing the sleeping men who so long have lain here amid these
   grotesque mounds.

Shrieking and screaming with terrifying humor,
howling their ghostly howls with despicable, arrogant, laughter,
like demons, they ride this watery world,
spilling its depths and creating havoc beneath its mighty swirl.

Their game over they soon retire
to disturb others in their ghostly attire.

6-14-67

The Stars

Beaming dots in the burning blue,
like diamond berets, they shine forever true.

A million years have come and gone,
but still the stars shine on and on.

Through countless eons, their mystery remains—
"The secret of the heavens"
unconquered, forever untamed.

Sparkling, twinkling, enchanting beauty bright,
magnificent delirious balls of light,
they pierce the blackest of angry nights.

Lighting the heavens with their ghostly array
like "gold-colored dewdrops" on a gloomy day,

the stars shine forever, always agleam,
as angels ever watchful, like fairies in a dream.

2-13-70

The Lament of the Dead

Far upon a lofty ridge, once oe'r it I did see
The wretched remains of a lonely man whose fate it had to be.

I suppose this lonely figure, a family man was he
But never again his loved ones were he ever to see.

I visualized the ancient courtroom where the verdict was brought
    down
Upon this doomed man then to earn his golden crown.

As I left the chalk dry bones lying in the gloom
it seemed that I could hear his tortured soul cry out to me.

But then all was silent: "cold icy fingers of stillness, there to be."

Evil's Incognito

In the deep dank shadowy gloom stalks a lone figure
his tattered cloak wrapped tightly about him
moving against the chilling winds,
ever moving against the chilling winds.
Shrieks, cries, fill the midnight air
while skeletons dance in the distance.
The night engulfs obscuring all view,
taking its toll of perilous hue.

The figure staggers through the dark night
all battered from falling, running scared in an awful fright.

The dawn breaks, bringing the light.
Evil forms flee in their blight.

The night fades into the morning light,
wiping out all traces of this evil night.

7-24-2009

Short Stories

A Small English Drama

I had just recently arrived in England via steamer. The next morning I got up early, for I had a headache. I hitched a ride to the apothecary in a lory. Stopping at a bistro, I had tea, rented a car, and looked in the boot of the motorcar for a beaker for more tea.

I ran low on petrol, so I stopped at a station for some and continued on my way. I decided to go to the cinema for some amusement and had to stop at the loo, after which I took my seat and enjoyed the picture. I spent several tuppence for treats while at the cinema. On the way back from the cinema, I stopped at a small out-of-the-way shop and bought an old gramophone and records, went to my room, and listened to them. Next morning I hopped in a hansom much later and enjoyed a trip down one of the city's many cobbled streets, for it was the early 1940s. There were still some of these old streets still there. I stopped at a letter-box, had some more tea and scones, then decided to call it a day. The next day I decided to do some more sight seeing.

So I wandered down another old street, saw this unusual cabinet, was very curious about it, so I bought it. Found out it was an old *Etagere*, a French cabinet, with open shelves.

Life is an adventure, and I was proving it in a small kind of way, wandering here and there, exploring one place and another. England has many moors. One can see them in old English cinema. There is an English song about a poor unfortunate unmarried girl and her child; the girl apparently froze to death on her father's doorstep, but the child lived. Imagine the poor father's horror the next morning, when he found her, because the poor man was deaf. These moors are surrounded by a heavy mist, which conjures up great mystery.

Another story is *The Hound of the Baskervilles*, about a hellish hound that roamed about preying on innocent victims. But it was finally tracked down and killed.

England has many horrible stories of torture and murder that defy description.

They are tourist curios now, but the locals say the poor victims' spirits still haunt many of these places. I stayed clear of all these sites,and continued on my way. I got tired of wandering about the city, got in a lift, retired for the night, got up the next morning, boarded an airship, and headed for the USA.

4-24-2009

The name of this old English song was called "Mary of the Wildmoor."

An English Story Using Their Words

It was a very fine day in "Merrie Olde Englande." We were riding in a motor-car räther fäst, hoping the bobbies wouldn't catch us.

On the way we passed by a wēir and saw a few motorboats as we motored along.

Then I developed an awful headache and had to go to the apothecary for some medicine.

We got back in the motor car and continued on our way. We decided to go to the pictures or cinema, ordered some fish and chips, and enjoyed the show. Later while motoring down one of England's old cobblestoned streets, we happened to run upon an old acquaintance. We talked with him for a little while then noticed it was getting late and there was a slight chill in the air, for it was mid September. We turned on a bit of heat, headed for the flat we had rented for the night, turned on the tele, and settled down for the night.

The next day bright and early, we got back in the motor car and continued sightseeing. We stopped at a little café and each had a beaker of tea and scones and sat there enjoying the scenery. We then got in a lift, rose five floors to our flat, read a bit, watched some tele, got tired, turned out the lights, and went to sleep.

A Curious Mystery

A Short Scottish Story

One day as I was strolling peacefully through Scottish country side, I saw a strange sight from afar. I hied[1] with a hod[2] and espied a cob[3] swimming in a tarn[4]. I got a drink of water from a large tun[5] that was in a basement of a towering castle that lay in the foothills of Scotland. Leaving there, I climbed a brae[6] that looked into the valley below.

I explored a little farther and there before me was a yawning chasm that seemed to beckon me to enter. As I stood there agog[7] at the gaping hole, billows of smoke began teeming[8] from the mouth of it. I gathered up enough courage to go into the grotto, and to my surprise there was no fire inside.

What was causing the smoke? I never found out.

The mystery deepened as I ventured farther into the dark dank[9] shadows of the cave. But it made no difference how far I went in. I never found the source of the smoke. Mystified at all this, I left there and never returned. I nicknamed the place "Ghost Valley."

8-06-09

Words used in the story and their meanings with diacritical markings.

---

1   *hīed—fled, ran*
2   *Hŏd—a coal scuttle*
3   *cŏb—male swan*
4   *Tärn—a small lake*
5   *Tŭn—a huge barrel*
6   *brāe—hillside*
7   *Ăgōg—standing with one's mouth open, awed, amazed!*
8   *Tēēming—pouring*
9   *dānk—wet, disgustingly damp*

24

The Unread Letter

Once when I was a small boy long ago, and while rummaging through an old house, as I often did back then, I came across this old trunk. It looked like it may have come over on an old ship in the 1600s. In it were many things, but the most mysterious of all was an old letter at the bottom.

It was unopened, sealed with wax, the way people sealed documents in the "dead days" of the past.

With trembling hand, I picked it up with overwhelming desire to open it, but I suppressed my desire and did not. For it had no name. A letter of great mystery—no address! Who was it to? What was in it? It looked very intriguing, for by the size of it contained many pages.

There it lay, its contents never to be revealed. For it was written by an "unknown hand," and great mystery surrounded it; it had no name, no address. Who could have written it? Why was it written? What was concealed in those long-forgotten pages? I put it back in the old dusty trunk, closed the lid, and walked away.

And there it still lies. Unless discovered by an uncaring intruder, it is still there, unopened, still sealed. Forevermore.

5-12-2008

The Forgotten Cathedral

The Tintinnabulation[10]! was near deafening as the many bells of an ancient cathedral rang and clanked from a high tower, as it was nearly hidden from view by the dense undergrowth that surrounded it. Its many windows were broken and smashed centuries ago by vandals.

The way the terrain was around it, it was like a giant chasm [11]that funneled the winds through its broken windows, causing the *bells* to emit eerie clinking sounds, as the ghostly winds whistled through its shattered panes.

Clinking, clanking, tolling, rolling, went the rusty voices of the lonely bells. Tolling rolling went the bells. I discovered this old cathedral one day while hiking by accident, as I was gathering wildflowers.

Time had almost forgotten the old cathedral, for its location was very treacherous. Like an old castle, it had a moat all around it, dug there after its worshippers abandoned it. Where water had once been, there was now just a deep ravine around the old cathedral, still trying to protect it from trespassers. For it was no longer a place of worship. It had been transformed into another place of endeavor. I somehow broke its taboo by laboriously scaling the almost impossible deep trench, finally making it to the top.

I cautiously crept up to the giant iron door, and with much creaking the heavy door did open. I went inside, and it was all in shambles from neglect and the weather. Broken glass was everywhere, lying shattered there on the floor.

I explored first one room and then another, but nothing but broken glass in every room. In the back of the titanic building I found the remains of an ancient clavichord, its strains long since silenced by time. The long pews lay there in perilous decay.

Then in almost a hidden niche of one room, I saw a great *iron* trunk. With much labour, I finally managed to open its heavy lid. Inside were many old books and scrolls of ancient texts, all written in the dead language of *Latin.*

---

10   *Tintinnabulation—ringing of many bells*
11   *Chasm—a deep ditch*

Forgotten, texts there in this old trunk did lie. Like "the unread letter" from another story of mine, I put them all back in the old trunk, closed the lid, and left them. Anyone else would have taken them.

All around everywhere, there were heaps of broken glass of the stained windows that once in the "forgotten cathedral" did dwell.

I left there headed back to civilization, and through the dark wood, and dense undergrowth, I could hear the *rusty-throated* knelling of the bells in the high tower, calling, echoing, resounding like the mythical handmaidens, the Valkeries[12] of the thunder god Thor, in their ghostly manner, soaring on a midnight wind.

The eerie pealing, knelling, tolling, rolling, clinking, clanking, ringing of the bells.

9/28/09

---

12   *Valkeries—mythical ghostly handmaidens of the Thunder God (Thor) of Greek mythology*

A Story of Hawaii

I had thought about it for a long, long time, but I never seemed to acquire the money for the trip. One day I finally got enough together and off I sailed for Hawaii. The voyage went well, with no trouble. Lasted about a week at sea, because we were on a slow steamer and had to lie in port some.

Finally I arrived on Hawaii's shore. There were *wahinins* (little maids with typical native attire) to greet us as we exited the ship. They put leis around our necks upon arriving, a native custom of the Islands. That night we dined on fish and poi, and were shown a grand time by our very gracious hosts. `

Next day I decided to do some sightseeing on my own. I saw volcanoes, where ancient sacrifices were made, and shuddered at the mere thought of it.

I left there, combed the beach for conch shells and crab. Found several, but left them, for they were too cumbersome to carry. Our troupe lingered there for a space of three weeks. The tour took in several interesting points of interest and places. There were ukulele strains and native bands that filled the air with entrancing revelry. There were tales of mystery, intrigue, as well as tales of terror that were told and retold.

Pearls of great price lie at the ocean's depth for divers who were brave enough to risk the perils of the deep to dive for them.

All this revelry and joy finally came to an end as we boarded ship, said a fond *aloha* to a beautiful Hawaii, and sailed for the mainland.

9-23-09

The Sea Monster

I had just arrived in England via steamer. As we exited the ship, I stopped at a local bistro for a spot of tea. As I sat sipping it, I noticed a frightful form through the window in the bistro, creeping through the dense fog that surrounded the little café.

As it drew nigher, I could see it was an ogre-like monster that maybe came up from the bowels of the sea. Panic spread everywhere as people began fleeing in all directions. The monster began to grow larger as it slithered down London's cobblestone street.

It crashed through a radio tower and demolished a couple of motor cars as it caused more damage to a nearby building.

It had one, big, red eye in the center of its head like a cyclops that acted like a telescope, and it was very radioactive. Actually, it was being consumed by the radioactivity. It roared in its muffled tone as it crept through the murky fog. The streets were completely bare as the monster went madly on its way, leaving a trail of slime in its wake.

What to do! What to do! Who could stop it? It seemed hopeless. The situation was very bad indeed. But all was not lost, for the lab boys labored anxiously searching for a solution to the dilemma.

Finally, they made a breakthrough, a machine that would dissolve the creature. Would the machine work?

Aiming it at the monster, they achieved success. The creature completely vanished with no residue, nothing.

All London breathed a sigh of relief as peace came once again to Londtontown. It all seemed like a nightmare.

Early the next morning, I boarded the steamer and headed back to the USA.

1-26-2010

The Tie and the New Car
A Tearful Christmas Story

It is the early 1940s, and the war is raging in Europe. Adolf Hitler wants to own the world. Here in the states, it is nearing Christmas, and there are these two brothers; they are wondering what to get each other for Christmas.

One was very successful and wealthy, the other very poor and crippled—a pitiful contrast. The big day came, and the rich brother invited his poor brother to his lavish party. Timidly, with the aid of a crutch, the poor brother hobbled into the great house.

Can you imagine his amazement when he saw all this finery, the dazzling lights, the beautiful Christmas tree, the fine furnishings? When all he had was a hut and one light in the ceiling? To him it must have seemed like a strange dream.

This sort of reminds me of my early childhood when I was in the first grade. We were sharecroppers, migrants, staying no more than three years at any one place. Christmas came and we drew names. When time came to give out presents, I received this beautiful toy car. It must have cost five dollars, a considerable sum of money for a toy in those days. All I could afford to give the other boy was a nickel pack of notebook paper and a penny pencil—six cents worth. I never will forget the look of disappointment on the boy's face when he saw the meager presents. I felt very badly, for we were very poor, and that was all Dad could afford. Poverty seemed to haunt us all through life.

Anyway, the two brothers meet. When time comes to give presents, the rich brother presents the poor one with this beautiful new car! All the other one could afford to give was this tie. Can you imagine how small he felt at this lavish affair? So out of place and with so small a gift? He just couldn't accept such a grand gift as this and left there.

They rarely saw each other after that, and the poor brother died. The other brother just tossed the tie in a drawer with all his other ascots, cravats, and numerous others. But he never knew this was a special tie, for it was sewn with fine gold. Even the clerk at the secondhand store never knew. There the tie lay, for it was made like any other tie and looked no different. No one ever knew about it until many years later, after the death of the rich one.

By and by, an auction was held and the tie was sold along with all the others.

The person who bought it was a collector of ties and must have sensed something very unusual about it that no one had ever noticed before.

As I said, the tie was very plain, very plain indeed. Upon careful examination of it, its fine splendor was finally revealed— worth a considerable amount of money. It was sewn with very fragile cloth, and the many years of being stored had worn away its fragile skin.

And when the buyer examined it so closely discovered his fine and rare prize. Who had owned it previously, no one ever knew. Even the smallest and seemingly insignificant things sometimes miraculously prove to be more valuable than the grandest.

12-08-09

Two Lonely Souls

Once upon a time, there was a little girl named Clara. You see, Clara was an orphan. She never knew kindness. Her parents both had been killed in war, for it was the mid-1800s. The orphanage where she grew up was very poor, and its caretakers were very mean to all the poor little waifs who lived there.

They were forced to work without any pay and with little food, and many of them died. Time went on, and Clara grew up. She was very afraid of people (a xenophobe). She was especially afraid of men, so she never married. She was a vagabond. She wandered here and there begging for food. People would chase her and say, "Be gone, you vagrant!" And Clara would spend many a long day lonely and blue. In the winter, she would huddle in a corner somewhere and hope some kind soul would find her and adopt her. But no one ever did.

When she became an old lady, good fortune at last smiled on her; she came into some money. She had a little house built at the edge of a green wood. Many pretty flowers surrounded the little house. There, she lived all alone, for she was afraid of men.

One day while sitting on the porch, a little wounded pup happened to wander by. Someone had shot it, and it could hardly walk. It cried piteously. Clara ran out to see if she could help it. It just lay there, faint from hunger pain.

Clara picked it up, took it inside, fed it, cleaned its wounds, and cared for it. It just lay there many days almost motionless. She thought the little pup would surely die but remained steadfast by its side and cared for it faithfully every day. With care and affection, the little dog began to get better. Weeks passed and Clara continued to stay by its side, caring for it, until it finally got well.

Time passed, and they grew very close, for each other was all they had. They were very happy in the little house by the edge of the green wood.

More time passed, and the poor woman died. She lay there many days before she was found. She had named the little dog Spot, and Spot thought she was just asleep. He was hungry because he hadn't been fed in many days. Like Clara when she was a little girl at the orphanage, it was all alone.

Hunger pains drove the little dog out into the world again since it was a pup. It wandered here and there, hoping for something to eat, but no one was kind to it. One old man threw a pot of boiling coffee at it, for it had disturbed him scratching at his door.

It never knew hardship, hunger, and cold since it was a hurt little pup because Clara had always cared for it, loved it, and because all they had was each other.

It wailed mournfully in the dark night. For it was very frightened. No one was kind to it. By and by, faint from hunger and neglect, the poor, homeless little creature, shivering and cold, died. Its little life was over. It lay there without a friend. So goes life. Two lonely souls, found and departed.

No happy ending to this sad tale.

Theories
and Dreams

Could These Theories Be the Answer Behind
The "Mona Lisa's Mystic Smile?"

One of two things . . . back in those days one never smiled in woodcuts or paintings. It would have been very *rare* indeed to see such.

The other is now; experts think the Mona Lisa isn't a woman at all, but Leonardo Da Vinci's *own* likeness.

So it was a *private* joke. And DaVinci *knew* it; and he was secretly, coyly, smiling at spectators, because he was so clever.

What If It Were Possible to Move Things by Sight?

If it were possible, say, to take the mind of a five-year-old child and advance it to such a state of growth so it could think like a full-grown adult, it might be possible to move things by sight. Levitation—that is the mind of a person of such a young age, totally uncluttered. Free! No sense of responsibility. Like the Bible says, "faith the size of a mustard seed." Think how small that really is. The trouble is mortals can't think that deep—too much doubt. We just can't think that freely—too many obstacles. But just think of what miracles we could do if only we could think that deeply.

5-14-2010

A Cure for Leprosy

I was watching this program on Channel 8 Friday night (April 4, 2008), sometime after 8 maybe 8:15, about this hospital in Louisiana. I think its name was *Caravelle*. It first started in 1896, and they were treating all these leper cases. To be called a leper (they said) was the most demeaning word you could dream of. So they called it Hanson's disease, because a man named Hanson first started working to try to find a cure for it. And he *did*!

They did it one way by placing these poor people in a "hot box," and bringing up their body temperature through heat. One poor man said it took four men to hold him down. No wonder the Bible said they were shut away. It showed people with hardly any face. There were big old hard crusts with holes in them all over their face, eyes, mouth, etc.

Many of these people died. But some of them were actually cured and released, and it showed them living and talking with normal lives today. It also said this disease (the modern way) was contracted from armadillos.

I don't know whether it would be available or not, but you might try calling Channel 8 TV in Nashville, Tennessee. A cure for leprosy—just imagine that here in the States! But I don't remember whether or not that hospital is still there, but you might could get a DVD of that program.

P.S. This hurt me so; I *cried* over it.

Our Corrupt Legal System
One Instance

I was watching this show on TV about this killer who murdered five elderly women and stole their purses and welfare checks. They (the *police* chased him). He threw the gun he used in a trash can. Due to some stupid law, just because when the garbage man put his garbage in the scoop of the garbage truck, and it wasn't mixed with the other garbage, they threw *all* the evidence out.

After he himself admitted to killing these five women, had *all* the evidence, the purses, the welfare checks, his finger prints on the gun, this stupid judge threw out all the evidence and the guy went free. He walked. Free! Just because they had no warrant to search a garbage can.

I guess it's true that all the laws these days are for the rotten criminals! How can this be? Furthermore, this same guy goes and murders a little boy.

The Cave

An Impossible Dream

I'm in this cave, and I see this image of a panther's face on a rock. It is turned sidewise, showing the profile of the beast.

I, for some reason, shove a rock in this face. It moves. It isn't on the rock but in it. There is a big hole in the rock, and the beast is inside it. I flee out of there. I can hear the growling of the panther as I make my hasty exit.

I run into another cave, but it is full of something like lint. A really weird thing occurs here. I see another face—that of a man on a round object, like a cylinder. I look at it and the eyes move! My sister Mildred is there and she picks up the object!

All of a sudden, there is a full-grown man standing there with one arm missing—a soldier. He is a WWII soldier, and he has a radio with him. Suddenly, it starts playing.

The scene shifts.

Now my sister, the soldier, and I are all in another room. The radio plays a record show of the 1940s. Nothing unusual in that, except the music coming out of the box isn't in our present time (rather out of the 1940s). The show is being broadcast live from the actual 1940s era, not 2015. While the soldier was in the cylinder, time froze, and he brought the past with him!

8-18-2015

Essays

Who We Are and Why We Are Different Each Day
An Essay

Have you ever wondered why everything looks different after you have been away for a while and come back? That is because you weren't there. You were somewhere else, and time of course was going on *there*. But you were somewhere else; not there. So it left a gap, a void.

And when you came back, you weren't the same person as you were when you left. You are somebody else. A different being. Aged a little, you have moved a tiny bit into the future.

Time passes a little every second, and it *changes us*. We all know that. You may not see it visibly, but it is there. If you really want to see evidence of this take a picture of yourself month by month and watch the change.

All of this is because of time (*Time!*). Nobody can stop it, turn it around, or even slow it down, and until God sees fit to end it, it will go on this way. Ruthlessly! Relentlessly!

Time *can* though be a friend or foe. It all depends on the situation.

I for one would like to make it stop. Just hold it, so it couldn't get away. Why things have to change in order for the world to progress, I have never been able to understand.

In today's world most things are made shoddy, ugly, and near useless.

Nothing lasts. There is no beauty in the world; especially what they call *entertainment*!

People in all forms of entertainment are half monster half robot, a bunch of wiseacre smart alecks, iconoclastic jerks, like they were programmed with no human aspect at all. It all comes down to this *change*! Who needs it!

Rewritten, Sunday, 10/19/08

A Sequel to
Who We Are, And Why We Are Different Each Day
An Essay

Like I said in the first "Who we are and why we are different each day" essay, even when an hour passes or a second, for that matter passes, we are *not* the same person, because we have passed a little further into the future. We are somebody different because of this thing called time. This aging process is ever changing us.

So that is why every day seems different than the day before. Especially if we have spent it somewhere else rather than at home.

We are all human beings, but God made us all different. If he had made us all the same then we would know each other's thoughts, habits, etc. Moreover we all would be like a bunch of robots with the same personalities. But we are not. So that makes us all different as we go through this life. Our cycle continues this change. Think how wonderful it would be if we could stop time for a while. Then there would be no change. We wouldn't age anymore unless we wanted to.

I wonder though if the stopping of time were possible and we could reverse the process. Would we be able to use our senses? Touch, hearing, smell, etc. Or would we only be spirits? Without any bodily form? Just think of that.

But of course it's impossible for now. And if the world continues to *be* and God allows it, someday we may be able to travel back in time and realize a lifelong dream. But that's too fantastic to even think about, even though our minds would like to think it possible. So I guess until "reverse time travel" becomes possible, we'll just have to be content the way we are.

July 30, 2009

Broken Blossoms
A 1919 Silent Movie Summary

There was this old 1919 silent movie I was watching Sunday night July 19, 2009, called *Broken Blossoms* that starred Donald Crisp as the meanest father I ever saw in any movie and little Lillian Gish as poor little Lucy.

In it she wandered around the waterfront the palest little waif anyone ever saw. Hoping somebody would be kind to her for her dad was so mean to her, for he would beat her for some failure of his, and she hardly ever smiled because she had such an awful home life.

Her Dad was a fighter. A real brute. And poor little Lucy was such a frail child, white as any ghost and frightened of almost everyone.

One day she ran away from home and fell in this Chinese shop where the "Yellow Man" in the movie owned and ran. She ran upstairs and collapsed on the floor. And there she lay.

By and by the "Yellow Man" came back to his shop, for he was away when little Lucy staggered in there. And he found her on the floor quivering from fright.

He treated her wounds, put such pretty garments on her, and fixed her lovely hair, and finally brought out her hidden beauty. Poor little Lucy, nobody had never been kind to her before, and she didn't know how to respond. Her little heart leaped with joy at the Chinaman's tender hand.

Then Evil eye, a spy in the movie, saw the little girl in the Yellow Man's shop, hastily he went and told the evil old father about it. The father hated anyone who wasn't from the states. In a rage, he stormed into the Chinese shop, wrecked the upstairs, and found his little girl.

He seized her, half dragged her to his apartment. She got away from him, and shut herself up in a closet.

This *really* made him mad. He glowered the meanest face that ever came on a human being. He was more mad animal than a man.

He grabbed a hatchet and started hacking away at the wooden door of the closet.

Poor little Lucy. This was the worst *heartwrenching* scene I dare say has ever been shown in any movie new or old. Little Lucy was so frantic. For she had no way to escape out of that closet. Fear just completely *engulfed* her. The splinters flew as the beast chopped away at the closet door.

He finally chopped through the door, seized little Lucy and literally beat his little girl to death. Hence part of the name of the movie the China Man had named her "White Blossom," because she was so pale, and had bird-like ways.

Poor little Lucy managed one little smile as she lay dying. The Yellow Man finally came back to his shop and found it wrecked and the little girl gone. He nearly went mad with grief. He lay there a little while writhing in anguish, grabbed his pistol, found where the beast was, and justifiably *shot* him.

He finally paid the full price here on earth for his brutal treatment of his little girl.

This hurt me so that I cried about it for over an hour. No one could have been that mean.

July 10, 2009

Youth: Just Exactly What Is It?

Youth, I guess, is almost impossible to describe fully. It is a magic age—an age when everything one sees is new, exciting, and free. Captured through a baby's eyes, it is just meaningless sights and sounds, yet a little baby's eyes light up, and they react to it.

As they get a little older, they get great joy out of things that make noise, like rattles, bells, and such.

Much later in our youthful existence, it is a land of butterflies in the stomach. Our imagination runs wild with all kinds of images and creations, and we have the desire to learn (for some of us) and to be somebody. We make our mark in the world, looking for that stamp of approval from the successful.

It is a time of great exploration, when the mind is free and uncluttered, a time to compose, to find ourselves, to really try to find out who we are and why we are here. It is a time to soar to new heights of learning, the church, the arts, and sciences.

It's the springtime of our early existence, a time to think of love and marriage and family (for some of us). It is a fantastic, incredible time that no artist could paint. It's too much to truly describe, surely, an age of magic.

CPSIA information can be obtained
at www.ICGtesting.com
Printed in the USA
JSHW032140131020
8750JS00001B/14